Headline Series

No. 282   **FOREIGN POLICY ASSOCIATION** $4.00

FRANCE
The Challenges of Renewal

by A.W. DePorte

1
France at 2,500 Years   3

2
The State and the Nation   6

3
The Wealth of the Nation   29

4
Promoting the National Interest   40

5
What's Next?   57

Talking It Over   62
Reading List   63

Cover Design: Ed Bohon
Photo: UPI/Bettmann Newsphotos

Jan./Feb. 1987
Published October 1987

The Author

A. W. DEPORTE was a career official of the U.S. Department of State for 25 years, where he served as a member of the policy planning staff and as director of the office of research on Western Europe. He is now a visiting scholar at the Institute of French Studies, New York University. He holds a doctorate in international relations from the University of Chicago. Dr. DePorte is the author of *De Gaulle's Foreign Policy, 1944–1946* (Cambridge, Mass., Harvard University Press, 1968) and *Europe Between the Superpowers: The Enduring Balance*, 2nd ed. (New Haven, Conn., Yale University Press, 1986).

The Foreign Policy Association

The Foreign Policy Association is a private, nonprofit, nonpartisan educational organization. Its purpose is to stimulate wider interest and more effective participation in, and greater understanding of, world affairs among American citizens. Among its activities is the continuous publication, dating from 1935, of the HEADLINE SERIES. The author is responsible for factual accuracy and for the views expressed. FPA itself takes no position on issues of U.S. foreign policy.

HEADLINE SERIES (ISSN 0017-8780) is published five times a year, January, March, May, September and November, by the Foreign Policy Association, Inc., 729 Seventh Ave., New York, N.Y. 10019. Chairman, Robert V. Lindsay; President, John W. Kiermaier; Editor in Chief, Nancy L. Hoepli; Senior Editor, Ann R. Monjo; Associate Editor, K. M. Rohan. Subscription rates, $15.00 for 5 issues; $25.00 for 10 issues; $30.00 for 15 issues. Single copy price $4.00. Discount 25% on 10 to 99 copies; 30% on 100 to 499; 35% on 500 to 999; 40% on 1,000 or more. Payment must accompany order for $8 or less. Add $1 for postage. Second-class postage paid at New York, N.Y. POSTMASTER: Send address changes to HEADLINE SERIES, Foreign Policy Association, 729 Seventh Ave., New York, N.Y. 10019. Copyright 1987 by Foreign Policy Association, Inc. Composed and printed at Science Press, Ephrata, Pennsylvania.

Library of Congress Catalog Card No. 87-82323
ISBN 0-87124-116-1

1

France at 2,500 Years

In 1987 the French people will note, if not celebrate, the thousandth anniversary of the dynasty that provided kings of France almost without interruption until 1848. The French know that 500 years before the dynasty was established the kingdom of the Franks had begun to emerge from an amalgam of Celts, Romans and Germans in the province of Gaul which Julius Caesar had conquered five centuries before *that*. Half a millennium earlier still, Greek colonists had founded Marseilles and had begun to draw the area that would be France into the orbit of Mediterranean civilization.

    This long and turbulent history is not just a memory but a "living" presence for the French of today to an extent that is unimaginable in most other countries. Their perception of themselves and their problems has deep roots in the past. The great moments of French history—the "June days" and the "July days," Thermidor and Brumaire, the Vendée and the commune—are well enough remembered, as fact or myth, to give a sharp undertone to current debates about the authority of the state, individual rights, the independence of the Catholic schools and the distribution of the national wealth among groups, classes and regions. Opponents of the proposal in 1946 to establish an all-powerful one-house parliament remembered France's previous experience with such a system: the Jacobin Convention of 1792-94 and its Reign of Terror. Objections in 1962 to the constitutional amendment providing for direct election of the president by the people rather than by an electoral college had roots in memories of Louis Napoleon Bonaparte's election in 1848 and his subsequent seizure of dictatorial power. The bloody suppression of workers' uprisings in 1848 and 1871 still colors labor-management relations today. French politics have a depth and intensity which surprise and exasperate peoples with shorter and less-divisive memories of their pasts.

France's history has also given its people a strong belief in their exceptional importance. The French were the most numerous people in Europe before the 19th century and had a long habit of thinking of their country as a leader among the nations. In the Middle Ages, France was the model feudal state. Later it was the model absolute monarchy and then the first large republic in Europe. Napoleon's armies controlled the continent (briefly) from Madrid to Moscow. Even when France did not dominate European politics, its civilization was widely admired and imitated. French was the language of diplomacy and "high culture" for centuries before World War II. Thomas Jefferson spoke for many when he said that France was "the most agreeable country on earth."

One of the major problems for the French of the 20th century has been to learn not to let internal quarrels rooted in the past limit their ability to deal with current issues. A second major problem has arisen from the fact that France is no longer the greatest power in Europe, nor is Europe any longer the center of the world. In an age of superpowers and emerging power centers in Asia, Africa and Latin America, the French have had to adapt their institutions and way of life to a world which they do not much like but with which they are irrevocably interdependent. The debate about what to change and what to preserve has been at the heart of France's politics since its shattering defeat by Germany in 1940. That defeat made change unavoidable if France were not to become a backwater of international life.

On balance, France has adapted well to the challenge. It remains important not only to the French but to the rest of the world. Its status may be diminished compared to the not-so-distant past but it remains a major international actor: one of five permanent members of the United Nations Security Council, one of five nuclear military powers, an active participant in the politics of Africa and the Middle East as well as of Europe. In addition it has become, at last, a modern industrial nation whose gross national product (GNP) is the fifth largest in the world and whose per capita income is among the dozen highest. Partly for that reason the traditional deep divisions of the French people along lines of ideology, class and religion have weakened. General Charles de Gaulle once said that the French left is against the state and the right is against the nation. These and other deep-rooted attitudes have by no means disappeared but they have not prevented institutions from being built—in the Fifth Republic—which, unlike those of most earlier French regimes, have been accepted as providing a legitimate framework for national decisionmaking. Change itself seems to have become less wrenching and more habitual to the French than in times past.

The French and others continue to debate how much France has lost or retained of its essential "French" characteristics as a result of the transformations it has experienced since World War II. In any case, the process of adaptation is far from complete, and is not likely ever to be insofar as the world of which France is a part continues to change rapidly. France has learned once again, in face of the economic dislocations of the last decade, that it must do more to keep up if it is not to fall back. If one had to make a prediction about the country's future, one might say that France would continue to be as troubled and troubling, creative and stimulating, as it has been at most periods of its long history, but also increasingly open to change as the inevitable condition of preserving what is best and most unique. Or, as Gertrude Stein, the American expatriate writer, put it: "It is nice in France they adapt themselves to everything slowly they change completely but all the time they know that they are as they were."

2

The State and the Nation

The French people ratified the constitution of the Fifth Republic by almost a four-to-one vote on September 28, 1958, and have lived under it ever since. The constitution was drafted under the direction of General Charles de Gaulle, who then became the Fifth Republic's first president. Many who voted for the constitution did not like the strong executive authority it created but believed that de Gaulle had to be given what he wanted because only he could extricate France from the anticolonial rebellion of Muslims against French rule in Algeria and the revolt of the French army there against the authority of the Fourth Republic. Some expected that once de Gaulle had restored military discipline and settled the Algerian problem, the familiar system of domination of the government by Parliament, and by the political parties that controlled it, would return, in practice if not in letter. In fact, however, the constitution not only survived the ending of the Algerian war (1962) and de Gaulle's resignation (1969) but has been consolidated by his conservative successors, Georges Pompidou (1969–74) and Valéry Giscard d'Estaing (1974–81), by the election of the first Socialist, François Mitterrand, to the presidency (1981), and by the election for the first time of a parliamentary majority politically opposed to the president (1986).

General Charles de Gaulle announced his resignation as first president of the Fifth Republic in 1969. The father of the present constitution, he had assumed the presidency in 1959.

French Embassy Press & Information Division

The constitution has thus proved to be not only adaptable to changing political circumstances but popular enough to reverse what had seemed, during the Third (1870–1940) and Fourth (1946–58) republics, to be a deep-seated French preference for parliamentary supremacy, notwithstanding the cabinet instability that apparently was inseparable from that system as practiced in France. (There were over 100 prime ministers under the constitution of the Third Republic and 22 under that of the Fourth.) The emergence and acceptance of a system of government that was democratic without being anarchic and stable without being authoritarian has been one of the most important changes in French politics—and political psychology—in recent years. It suggests that the Fifth Republic's constitution, flexibly applied, has become respected enough to remain in place indefinitely.

The very name of the regime, however, reminds us that four

other French republics have come and gone over the years, along with several forms of monarchy. The present constitution is the 15th France has had since the revolution of 1789. The fact that it has already lasted longer than all except one of them (the Third Republic) promises well for its survival. But the fact that all previous French regimes collapsed in the face of revolution (1830, 1848) or foreign defeat (1814, 1815, 1870, 1940) or internal coup or convulsion (1792, 1794, 1799, 1851, 1958) reminds us that every one of them—even the long-lived Third Republic—failed to acquire the legitimacy or public support necessary to allow it to survive extraordinary challenges.

General de Gaulle, the father of the present regime, is the dominant figure in 20th-century French history. In June 1940, as an army brigadier-general and deputy minister of war in the last democratic cabinet of the Third Republic, he refused to accept the defeat of France by Germany. With the boldness and courage that marked his long career, he challenged the collaborationist government set up by Marshal Henri Philippe Pétain in unoccupied France and raised the banner of Free France. Almost alone at first, from London, and later Algiers, he inspired and led the French resistance against the Pétain regime and the Germans. In August 1944 he returned to liberated Paris as head of a new regime. But his attempt to create a constitutional system that would differ from that of the Third Republic by providing for a strong executive power alongside the Parliament was rejected by the political parties. He resigned from office in 1946, returning only in 1958 when the Fourth Republic broke down in face of the Algerian war and the military rebellion which it provoked. His price for returning to power in those difficult circumstances was to be given authority by the existing Parliament to draft a new constitution, subject to popular ratification. His strong leadership dominated the new system of government for 10 years, and he bequeathed to his successors a model of presidential control that enabled them also to dominate policymaking.

The election of François Mitterrand to the presidency in May 1981 for a seven-year term and the success of his Socialist party in winning a majority of seats in the National Assembly in June—

National Assembly Elections

	June 14, 1981		March 16, 1986	
	Percentage of Votes	Seats	Percentage of Votes	Seats
Communists (PCF)	16.12	44	9.78	35
Socialists (PS) and allies	37.77	285	31.04	216
Rally for the Republic (RPR)	20.91	88	40.98	148
Union for French Democracy (UDF)	19.16	63		129
National Front (FN)	—	—	9.65	35
*Total		491		579

*The totals include small parties and unaffiliated deputies. The number of seats was increased between 1981 and 1986. The RPR and UDF ran joint lists of candidates in 1986 but those elected formed separate groups in the National Assembly.

something achieved only once before by any party—marked a sharp shift of political control in France away from the previous conservative leadership. But it made no difference in the way the institutions worked. The new president had as firm control of the National Assembly through his victorious party as any of his predecessors had ever had. Mitterrand and the Socialists had formerly criticized the constitution and talked of amending it, but once in office they operated just as previous presidents and majorities had done.

Socialist Rule

President Mitterrand's double success was the culmination of a long and checkered political career. An eloquent intellectual, member of the resistance and veteran politician of the Fourth Republic, in which he had been left of center but not a Socialist, he had opposed the new constitution in 1958 and run a respectable race against de Gaulle in the 1965 presidential election. His assumption of leadership of the moribund Socialist party in 1972 and his development of an opportunistic alliance with the then stronger Communist party seemed for many years unlikely to shake the seemingly permanent rule of the right. Yet in 1981 the Socialists not only achieved that goal but also reduced the Communists to subordinate members of the alliance of the left—an achievement that Mitterrand considers one of his most important successes.

The Socialists interpreted their victory as giving them a clear mandate as well as the unchallengeable power to implement the broad changes in government policy and French society they had promised. Mitterrand, it is true, had won only about 26 percent of the vote in the first round of the presidential election. He owed his 52 to 48 percent victory over Giscard d'Estaing in the runoff not only to those who had voted for the Communist candidate but to the support (or abstention) of a swing group of voters who had preferred Jacques Chirac, the candidate of the Gaullist party, and were anti-Giscard rather than pro-Socialist in their sentiments. Some of the votes and abstentions which made possible the massive Socialist success in the subsequent parliamentary elections also no doubt reflected a traditional voter preference for giving the president control of the National Assembly rather than positive support for Socialist policies. Nevertheless, the two parties of the left had won 54 percent of the vote and the Socialist party had won a large majority of the seats. Understandably the Socialists, who had been out of office for more than 20 years and had never before enjoyed such a victory or grant of power, were determined to seize this perhaps unique opportunity to carry out the changes they thought necessary.

Their program was ambitious. For many years they had claimed that they, unlike the social democrats of northern Europe, would not be content once in office merely to modernize and reform the capitalist system, but would carry out a decisive "rupture" with it and build a new socialist society. There was nothing totalitarian or antidemocratic in their design but rather a belief that nationalization of a substantial part of the economy,

French Embassy Press & Information Division

CHANGE AND CONTINUITY IN FRANCE
Maquette of the controversial glass pyramid by the American architect I. M. Pei in the court of the Louvre

the introduction of new forms of labor-management relations, decentralization of the administration of the highly centralized French state and measures to help the less advantaged would make French society more just and democratic and the French economy more productive.

The centerpiece of the Socialist programs enacted between 1981 and 1986 was the nationalization, beginning in February 1982, of six major industrial groups, two financial groups and some three dozen banks and the purchase by the state of a majority or controlling block of shares in several other industrial and financial companies. (The Socialist government's economic policies as well as its foreign and defense policies are discussed more fully in later chapters.) In addition, the government increased the minimum wage, family benefits, old-age pensions and health care; required a fifth week of paid vacation; reduced the retirement age to 60 years and the workweek to 39 hours; enacted a set of laws (named for Jean Auroux, the minister who sponsored them) designed to increase the role of workers in the management of their workplaces; abolished the death penalty and reformed the criminal justice system, including termination of the special Court of State Security; and increased the authority of local administrations in a historic attempt to reverse the seemingly eternal trend toward ever greater centralization of power in the French state. Prime Minister Pierre Mauroy called decentralization "the main business of the presidential term."

The Socialist government also gave much emphasis and considerable resources to cultural policy, which included two projects of symbolic as well as practical importance: the building of a new opera house at the historic Place de la Bastille in a working-class area of Paris and the erection of a boldly modern glass pyramid, designed by an American architect, as the conspicuous new entrance to France's greatest museum, housed in the classic palace of the Louvre.

It is not clear yet what will be the long-term effects of decentralization on administration and politics or of the Auroux laws on labor-management relations and whether these changes will meet their proponents' expectations. There are indications, for example, that some employers have been able to apply the Auroux laws in ways less favorable to the labor unions than intended. Much more important for the reputation of the government in the near-term was its attempt to reduce unemployment by stimulating the economy. The effect of its policies was to push the French trade and payments balances into heavy deficits. This led, in turn, to three devaluations of the franc and the introduction in March 1983 of an austerity program that diminished inflation but at the cost of increasing unemployment. This was a particularly painful development for a government of the left.

The Socialists began losing parliamentary by-elections as early as January 1982, even before the effects of their economic policies had become clear. But their record of economic management, particularly when measured against Socialist promises, did more than anything else to erode the popularity of the president and the party. Militant supporters felt betrayed by the government's retrenchment policies and its sudden praise of a "mixed economy" as the answers to France's problems, while militant opponents were not appeased by what they considered its belated "realism." Socialist weakness was confirmed by every poll and by the municipal elections in March 1983, the elections to the European Parliament in June 1984 and the departmental elections in March 1985.

The government's problems were not only economic. Its attempt to satisfy the strong anticlerical wing of the Socialist party by increasing state control over government-subsidized private schools (mostly Roman Catholic) reactivated an ancient and very divisive debate and provoked large demonstrations in June 1984. The government chose to back down on its proposals. Later the same year it seemed to let itself be duped into unilaterally withdrawing French forces from Chad in return for a promise Libya later broke to do the same. In 1985 it was revealed that the government had authorized intelligence agents to blow up a ship belonging to Greenpeace, an environmental protection group, in a New Zealand port, presumably to prevent its entering the waters of French Polynesia to protest the testing of nuclear weapons. These and other episodes, which for many cast doubt on the government's ability to govern, did nothing to counter the political impact of its economic policies.

The Socialists did better than many expected in the March 1986 elections for the National Assembly, but no one was surprised that they lost their majority to a conservative coalition made up mainly of the Gaullist party, the Rally for the Republic (RPR), led by former prime minister Jacques Chirac, who is also mayor of Paris, and the Union for French Democracy (UDF), a looser grouping including former president Giscard d'Estaing, former prime minister Raymond Barre, and minister of culture François Léotard. (See table on page 9.) In 1981 power had passed, for the first time under the Fifth Republic, from one political bloc to another. In 1986 it passed back, but only partially. For the first time the constitution had to accommodate a situation that had long been anticipated and feared: a president of one political persuasion and a majority in the National Assembly of another.

President, Prime Minister and Parliament

Suddenly it became clear that presidential domination of the system had not been based on the authority assigned to the president by the constitution. Rather, it was based on the fact that all presidents until then had been able to join the powers of their office with those of the prime minister, whom they appoint, because they themselves controlled a majority in the National Assembly, to which the prime minister is responsible. Once President Mitterrand lost that control he had little choice but to name a leader of the new majority as prime minister: the dominant parties would accept no one else. He yielded to the logic of the election results by picking, or accepting, Chirac, leader of the largest conservative party. Dominance thus shifted to the Assembly, that is, to the prime minister who is the leader of its majority bloc. His policies reflect his coalition's preferences, not the president's. The imperial presidency practiced by de Gaulle and his successors thus came to an end, at least until such time as the president again gains control of the Assembly. A new phase of power-sharing began, which the French call cohabitation.

This political shift drew renewed attention to the constitution, which functioned in a very different way after March 1986 than it had before. It became apparent that the document did not, after all, create a presidential regime in the American manner. While it did much to strengthen the executive authority as compared to what it had been before and to curtail the role of Parliament, it divided executive power between the president of the republic and the prime minister.

In some ways this two-headed executive resembled the arrangements that prevailed in the 19th-century constitutional monarchies. The president, as chief of state, symbolizes national unity, sees to "the regular functioning of the public powers as well as the continuity of the state" and exercises a vaguely defined special influence with respect to foreign policy and national defense. The French president, however, is not a hereditary

Cohabitants: French voters in 1986 elected a conservative Parliament, led by Prime Minister Jacques Chirac (left) to share power with Socialist President François Mitterrand, whose party had ruled since 1981.

monarch but a partisan leader—in fact, if not always in name—who is elected (since 1962) by direct vote of the people and vested with the prestige that this national mandate gives him. His powers are substantial. The most important, besides naming the prime minister, include the authority to dissolve the National Assembly (presumably with the hope that a new one would be more amenable to his control or at least would have a coherent majority), to refer certain legislation to popular referendum on the proposal of the government, and, in extreme emergencies, to take over total control of the state for as long as he thinks it necessary. (The example of the crisis of June 1940, when the president sat silent as the cabinet decided to surrender to Germany, is usually recalled in this connection.) The president is also "chief of the armies" and has authority to "press the button" to launch France's nuclear weapons.

The French chief of state is not, however, as in the United States, also chief of government. The government, under the constitution, consists of the prime minister and the members of his cabinet whom he nominates and the president names. It is empowered to "make and conduct the policy of the nation." When the president does not control the party or parties that have a majority in the National Assembly, then they, and not he, control the government and, with it, policymaking.

The political situation as it existed in France before March 1986 produced essential harmony between the branches of government for 27 years and obscured the extent to which the constitution laid the base for possible conflict. The political situation since then has shown the flexibility of the document with respect to cohabitation but has also exposed its potential as a source of institutional discord. The fact that the president's term is for seven years (a relic of the politics of the 1870s which became a habit) and the National Assembly's is for five (unless dissolved by the president, as in 1981, before its time) increases the prospect of conflict. This is so because between the president and the deputies, who can be elected in different phases of the national political mood, stand the prime minister and cabinet. In 1981 the new Socialist president got around this difficulty by dissolving the conservative National Assembly elected in 1978 and giving the voters the opportunity, a few weeks after they elected him, to choose a new Assembly. In the 1986 legislative elections, however, the voters had no reason to think that Mitterrand would resign if his party lost control of the National Assembly and they showed that they were willing to accept the consequences of electing an Assembly majority which was not on the same side of the political spectrum as the president.

Whether the president or the prime minister dominates policymaking, the constitution was carefully shaped to circumscribe the role of Parliament, and particularly that of the more important lower house, the National Assembly, which had dominated the political scene during the Fourth Republic and often treated the ephemeral cabinets of the day as little more than its executive committee. Thus, Parliament can sit only at precisely and narrowly defined times and (according to a precedent set by de Gaulle in apparent contradiction to the letter of the constitution) cannot call itself into special session unless the president agrees. The government controls the agendas of both the National Assembly and the upper house, the Senate. It has authority to enact its proposed budget if Parliament does not adopt a budget within a given time period. While Parliament has sole power to enact laws (there is no presidential veto as in the United States), it can legislate only on topics listed by the constitution. The government issues regulations with the force of law on all other subjects.

The constitution established a new body, the Constitutional Council, to keep Parliament from overstepping these limits. It can also pronounce on the constitutionality of laws before they are promulgated, if asked to do so by the president, the prime minister, the president of either house of Parliament, or (since 1974) 60 members of either house. The Constitutional Council used this power sparingly before 1981 but with considerable vigor since then to strike down a number of important laws.

The most powerful weapon of the National Assembly (not shared by the Senate) is its ability to dismiss the cabinet provided that a majority of all the deputies votes for a motion of censure. The constitution gives an ingenious twist to this traditional power of the National Assembly by providing that, whenever the cabinet decides to declare that the vote on a proposed bill will be the equivalent of a vote of confidence, the legislation is considered to have been enacted unless a motion of censure is adopted. This means that bills can be passed without ever having been voted on if no such motion is presented within a given time. Even if a motion of censure with respect to a bill is presented, there may be some deputies who would like to defeat the bill but will not vote for censure (thus in effect voting against it, since only votes in favor are counted) because they do not want to take responsibility for ousting the cabinet. This would be particularly likely if they have reason to fear that defeat of the cabinet would lead the president to dissolve the Assembly and force the deputies to face the voters.

Such a dissolution has taken place only once, in 1962. It led to de Gaulle's victory over the short-lived majority that had challenged him, after the ending of the Algerian war, by ousting his prime minister.

Even by himself the prime minister is thus in a position of strength which his many predecessors in the Third and Fourth republics would have envied (if they had not thought that such power was undemocratic). When he and the president work together they have a formidable array of weapons with which to get their programs adopted by Parliament and to block legislation they do not like. As a result the cabinet instability that characterized earlier regimes has become a distant memory. The four presidents of the Fifth Republic have appointed only 10 prime ministers in 28 years. The 10 governments have had their problems even with politically congenial majorities in the National Assembly, but on the whole they have been able to enact the programs and implement the policies that they desired.

The existence of this system of strong government has not meant, however, that the venerable French tradition of direct action by aggrieved groups against unpopular policies is dead. Presidents and governments with firm control of the National Assembly have sometimes found it politically prudent to alter their legislative programs in the face of demonstrations in the streets. This was the case in 1984 with the Socialist government's attempt to strengthen state control over Catholic schools and in 1986 with the Chirac government's attempt to revamp the university system. Under the Fifth Republic, such episodes have sometimes forced policy changes even on strong governments but they have never gone so far as to provoke the collapse of the regime or even to drive a president or prime minister from office. (The possible exception was the student and labor demonstrations known in France as the "events" of May–June 1968, which launched a chain of circumstances leading to de Gaulle's resignation the next April after losing a referendum on decentralization.) The ability of the political leaders and system up to now to accommodate these extraconstitutional pressures does not prove that such will always be the case. But at least it can be considered a sign of the adaptability of the institutions, which can seem so strong as to risk being dangerously inflexible.

Political Parties

The success of the constitution has contributed to, and been reinforced by, changes in the French party system since 1958. Among the most significant of these have been the virtual disappearance of the two centrist parties of the Fourth Republic, the Radical-Socialists and the Popular Republican Movement (MRP), which provided 15 of the 23 chiefs of government who served between de Gaulle (1945) and de Gaulle (1958), and the resulting structural polarization of politics between a more or less permanent alliance of the two main parties on the right of the political spectrum (the RPR and the UDF) and a Socialist party on the left which in the 1980s has been stronger than either but less strong than both and cooperates intermittently with a Communist party (PCF) now in sharp decline.

These and other developments reflect a complex mix of political factors, including issues, leaders and changes in society affecting the clienteles of the various parties. The urbanization and secularization of the country since World War II, for example, almost inevitably had a negative impact on the Radical-Socialist party, which represented farmers and the business and professional people of small-town France, and the MRP, supported by Roman Catholics.

Changes in party strength were also influenced by changes in the election laws. The system adopted by the de Gaulle government in 1958 provided that the country would be divided into hundreds of districts, as in the United States, each of which would elect one deputy. But if no candidate won a majority of all the votes cast (which rarely happened in multiparty France), a runoff would be held in which only a plurality of votes was needed to win the seat. All the candidates were allowed to run again except those who received less than 12.5 percent of the vote. In practice, however, less-well-placed candidates of parties of the right and left usually withdrew from the runoff and threw their support to better-placed candidates of more or less similar political persuasion. (Gaullist and UDF candidates would withdraw for each other, as would Socialists and Communists.) A cliché of French politics is that on the first round the citizens vote for the candidate they like best, but in the runoff they vote for whomever is in the best position to defeat the candidate they like least.

One effect of this system in the political circumstances of the Fifth Republic has been that the smaller parties (both centrist and extremist) would win a smaller proportion of seats than of votes because fewer of their candidates would "place" or "show" in the first round of voting than those of the large parties. A second effect has usually been to give the coalition getting the most votes—the right in every election except that of 1981—a larger proportion of seats in the National Assembly than the proportion of votes cast for its candidates. This, in turn, helped produce cohesive governing majorities in the Assembly, an outcome that was foreseen.

Before the 1986 elections the Socialists, who feared just such a "magnified" victory by the right, replaced the 1958 law with a system of proportional representation. Their calculation proved correct. The two main parties of the right did not win a "magnified" majority but had only four more seats in the Assembly than the combined opposition, in part because proportional representation allowed Jean-Marie Le Pen's far-right National Front (FN) to win 35 of the 579 seats with 9.6 percent of the total vote. Most of those seats would probably have gone to the RPR or UDF on the runoff ballot if the previous system had been in effect. The Chirac government has now restored the 1958 law with the hope of winning a larger majority of Assembly seats for the conservative coalition in the next election, in 1991 or sooner, by containing the FN and frustrating a revival of independent centrist parties.

The decline of the centrist parties after 1958 and the move of many of their former voters toward one or another party of the right consolidated the long-term ascendancy of the conservative side of French politics. At the same time, the differences between the two main parties on the right diminished, for all the noisy leadership quarrels within and between them. The old-line conservatives who had thought Gaullism both undemocratic and too modernizing were largely replaced after the 1962 political crisis by a younger generation, led by Giscard d'Estaing, who accepted the Gaullist regime and most of its works but chose to keep a separate political identity. They distanced themselves from the Gaullist party more for tactical reasons than because of large policy differences. Gaullism itself, as represented by the party that claims descent from the general, has evolved since his time. Some of de Gaulle's most controversial policies, including creation of a national nuclear force, have been accepted by nearly everyone. Other policies, including his hostility to an integrated Western Europe and his kind of permanent challenge to U.S. "hegemony" in the Western alliance, faded away to a point where they ceased to be obstacles either to the recruitment of centrist voters or to regular cooperation, at the polls and in government, between the RPR and other parties of the right and center-right.

On the left, the decline of the Communist party reflects long years of rigid and unappealing Stalinist leadership and failure to democratize the party. It also reflects a decline in the size of its basic working-class constituency, their class consciousness and their loyalty to the party. A mood of anti-Sovietism has come over France in recent years, stimulated first by belated attention to the realities of the Soviet police state (the "Solzhenitsyn syndrome") and strengthened by Soviet policies toward Afghanistan and Poland. There has been a widespread turning away from Marxist ideas, particularly among intellectuals. The Communists have also been hurt by the rebirth of a dynamic and successful Socialist party led by François Mitterrand. Neither cooperation with the Socialists (1972–77), nor hostility toward them (1977–81), nor a last minute realliance in 1981 and the participation of four Communists in the Socialist-led cabinet, followed by their resignations in 1984, prevented a continuous decline in Communist voting strength from a high of 22.5 percent in the 1967 National Assembly elections to 20.6 in 1978, 16.1 in 1981 and 9.8 in 1986.

The overall weakening of the Communist party's position has helped the Socialists who, even after their policy turnaround in 1982–83 and their defeat in 1986, remain the largest electoral force in France. Non-Socialists have found it easier to vote Socialist sometimes (as in 1981, when they were dissatisfied with an incumbent conservative president) because they are less concerned about the influence the Communists might exercise in or on a government of the left. The Communists' role in government between 1981 and 1984 and their subsequent loss of almost 40 percent of their voting strength have probably reinforced such thinking.

The 1981 election showed that the right, though it is both larger and more nearly homogeneous than the left, cannot win every election. Issues and leaders can make a difference, particularly in presidential elections, where the perceived image of "the man" is important. The outcome of the presidential race can then have further important effects on the other parts of the system, as in 1981. It has also become clear since then that the constitution is workable for a president and majority of the left as well as of the right. What had seemed unthinkable or even unnatural to some on the right (and even on the left) became normal. The outcome of the 1986 elections provided another important lesson: that the dominance of the president can be ended if a National Assembly majority in opposition to him is elected and he decides, for constitutional or tactical political reasons, to choose the prime minister from among the leaders of the new majority, however hostile they may be to him and his policies.

Cohabitation was welcomed by the public at first as the players limited their confrontation, but became less popular as they increasingly maneuvered for advantage in the presidential election that will take place no later than April 1988. The new majority in the National Assembly has been able to enact its program notwithstanding the narrowness of its control and the president's sometimes muted, sometimes active, opposition. But everyone has understood that the period between the National Assembly elections of March 1986 and the presidential election is an interim. It will end when the public, by voting for one or another candidate on the basis of personality and economic and other issues, places full executive and legislative power in the hands of the right or, again, of the Socialists, or imposes some version of the kind of cohabitational arrangement that was created in 1986.

The Return of the Right

The government formed after the 1986 election did not set only interim goals for itself. Nor did it promise a return to the policies of its conservative predecessors in the 1970s. On the contrary, the RPR and UDF announced "projects" and "propositions" for the transformation of France which in their way seemed as ambitious and ideological as those the Socialists had advocated in 1981. The Chirac government did not challenge decentralization, or abolition of the death penalty, or longer vacations or the shorter workweek, or the social benefits enacted by the Socialists. But the core of its program was economic change: an effort to stimulate growth, competitiveness and exports and to reduce unemployment by cutting back on the state's role in the economy and thereby unleashing private initiative from government-imposed constraints and burdens. The new government, described by André Fontaine in *Le Monde* as the first since World War II to "recognize itself as of the right," was more inspired by what it found appealing in "Reaganism" and "Thatcherism" than by the record of previous conservative governments. The latter—and not least de Gaulle's—were usually more "Colbertist" (from Louis XIV's finance minister, who regulated trade and industry in the interest of the state) than "liberal" (in the French sense of the word which, unlike the American, means freeing business and the economy to a considerable extent from government controls).

The Chirac government, notwithstanding its narrow majority in the National Assembly, undertook to denationalize over several years not only the many companies taken over by the state in 1982 and after but also a number of those nationalized soon after World War II. In addition, it took steps meant to encourage investment and make it easier for business to hire and fire without government authorization. The parties in the Chirac government know that these policies are long-term and, in the best of circumstances, will have only limited effects on the economy by the time of the 1988 election. But they hope that the results with respect to growth and the foreign trade and payments balances will be sufficiently satisfactory—at least when compared to the Socialists' record—to allow them to claim that their economic policies are on the right track. (See Chapter 3.) They admit, though, that unemployment will remain high.

The problem of foreign immigration—or, more precisely, the place of immigrants and their children in French society—is clearly less important than the issues raised by the restructuring of the national economy. But politicians do not always choose their own priorities, and the conservative parties, responding to voter concerns, have given the immigration issue a high place in their campaigns and on their policy agendas.

In recent years a significant part of the French public has become preoccupied with such questions as whether there are too many foreigners living in France, what access they should have to social benefits and political rights, and in what circumstances they and their children who are born in France should be allowed to become French citizens. They allege that immigrants are taking jobs away from the French and are responsible for an undue proportion of crime. But not all foreigners are blamed. The many Iberians and Asians living in France are much less unpopular than immigrants from France's former dependencies in North Africa (Tunisia, Algeria, Morocco) and, to a lesser extent, those from black Africa and the West Indies.

All political parties have had to pay attention to the twin issues of immigration and crime. But they have been exploited most effectively by the National Front, headed by Jean-Marie Le Pen, a veteran of Pierre Poujade's demagogic movement of the 1950s in defense of small business and of the struggle to keep Algeria French. Le Pen has been remarkably successful in using the immigration and crime issues to win votes (from 8 to 11 percent in four elections between 1983 and 1986) and set the national agenda on the immigration question. His success is the more remarkable in light of his failure until 1981 to get anywhere with nationalist themes drawn from the usual armory of the extreme right. Something about the political situation in the 1980s, with the left in power, increasing unemployment and other economic distress, gave the immigration issue, and Le Pen's call for reducing the number of North Africans in France, a wider audience than it or he had found before.

While some of the FN's support has come from former Communist and other voters on the left, more has come from the right, notably those in urban areas where large numbers of immigrants live. The RPR and UDF understood that they had to do something about the immigration issue in order to win back as many FN voters as possible. This has been particularly important for Prime Minister Chirac because he fears that Le Pen, who has announced that he will seek the presidency in 1988, might draw away enough of his own potential support on the first round of the voting to allow his rival Raymond Barre to run best among the conservative candidates.

The new government therefore took steps to tighten control of entry into France and of foreigners in it. The administrative procedures for expelling immigrants found to be in the country illegally were simplified despite objections that this would subject them to summary expulsion. The heart of the issue, however, is the status of the large number of children born in France to noncitizens. The government proposed amending the nationality code to suspend automatic citizenship for such persons by reason of birth. Instead, when they were between 16 and 21 years of age they would have to ask for citizenship and demonstrate a knowledge of French appropriate to their job or profession. Proponents of the proposal said citizenship should be given only to those children of noncitizens who expressly wanted it and could show that they were capable of being assimilated into French society. Critics argued that in principle it would substitute what amounted to a racial definition of being French for the long-established policy of accepting as such anyone born on French soil. In practice it would subject immigrants' children who sought citizenship to arbitrary and probably discriminatory procedures. By delaying the granting of citizenship and making it uncertain, the proposed law, it was said, would relegate children of immigrants to an officially sanctioned limbo for many years and make their integration into society more difficult.

In reaction to this opposition, the government withdrew the proposed legislation from Parliament for further study. But all French political parties, and particularly the RPR and UDF, continue to wrestle with the immigration problem, which concerns much of the French public at a time of high unemployment and low population growth. Le Pen's appeal appears to have survived the efforts of the Chirac government to win over his followers by responding not only to their concerns with respect to immigration but also security (promises to "terrorize the terrorists") and "family values" (a widely ridiculed crackdown on allegedly pornographic publications by Charles Pasqua, the "law and order" minister of the interior). Le Pen continues to draw the support of 10 percent or more in opinion polls. Having failed to weaken his appeal, the leaders of the majority parties, beginning with Chirac, now face the unappealing alternative of having to do business in some way with Le Pen himself if they are to get the votes of his followers in future elections. What might his price be? Some speculate that he wants not only immigration legislation to his taste but also a cabinet position, perhaps as minister of defense.

The "law and order" government's backing down on an issue of much political importance for its leaders coincided with the withdrawal of other important proposed legislation in the face of unexpected—and extraparliamentary—opposition. Its plan to reorganize higher education, a permanent issue for all governments, provoked street demonstrations in late 1986 by large numbers of university and secondary school students after many years of political somnolence. The death of a student of North African background during a demonstration so stiffened opposition to the proposed legislation and to the government's handling of the issue that the minister of higher education found it prudent to resign, and the proposal was withdrawn from Parliament.

With unemployment high and the unions weak, French labor had also been quiet for several years. The success of the student action emboldened railway, electricity and Paris transportation workers to go out on strike in January 1987 more or less spontaneously, without union leadership. In this case public

Raymond Barre, an independent conservative and former prime minister, is expected to make a bid for the presidency in 1988.

French Embassy Press & Information Division

opinion eventually turned against the strikers, who were disrupting essential public services, and the work stoppages ended with compromise agreements on the issues in question. But the episode, coming so soon after the clash with the students, raised further question about the government's competence in pursuing policies which estranged large sectors of society.

Since competence has been one of Chirac's claims to political attention, the record of his troubled second term as prime minister has not smoothed his path to becoming the dominant leader of the right and, as such, his ascent to the presidency. Chirac has been a dynamic and successful politician, but he also has many opponents. In 1974, after the death of President Pompidou, he supported Giscard for the presidency rather than the candidate of his own Gaullist party. Giscard then made him prime minister and he took over the leadership of the Gaullists. In 1976, however, Chirac resigned as prime minister and in 1981 he ran against Giscard for president. On the runoff ballot he did not discourage his supporters from voting for Mitterrand or abstaining, thus contributing to Giscard's defeat and the Socialist victory. It is not surprising, therefore, that Chirac's difficulties have been welcomed not only by the Socialists but by many members of his own coalition.

One beneficiary of Chirac's problems has been his principal rival on the right, Raymond Barre, a professional economist who replaced him as prime minister during the second part of Giscard's presidency. Barre is a member of the National Assembly but not of the government. He has a much less combative image than Chirac and fewer enemies, is more reassuring to centrists, and is remembered favorably by those who want to reduce the government's role in the economy for having initiated policies to that end while he was prime minister. Barre is thus in a good position to get the support in 1988 of conservative and centrist voters who do not like one or another aspect of Chirac's policies or leadership.

Polls suggest that the Socialist party has also recovered much of its popularity as the Chirac government has lost ground. President Mitterrand or, if he decides not to run, some other Socialist seems well placed to give either Chirac or Barre a close race.

3

The Wealth of the Nation

The French economy has been "in crisis" throughout the 1980s. In 1981 the parties of the left made a campaign issue of the fact that the economic growth rate was too low (1.1 percent in 1980) and unemployment too high (6.4 percent). In 1986 the parties of the right, in turn, said that growth in 1985 was still too low (1.4 percent) and unemployment much higher (10.2 percent). Each offered prescriptions for France's problems—socialism in the one case, liberalism (as the French define it) in the other—and each in turn won elections in which economic issues were dominant.

The economic expectations of the 1980s in France are very different from those of earlier years. During the 1960s the French annual economic growth rate averaged 5.8 percent, which was ahead of that of West Germany (4.7 percent), the United States (4.0 percent) and Britain (2.7 percent). Most of the industrialized countries grew more slowly in the 1970s, in part because of the rise in energy prices following 1973. Even so, French growth averaged 3.7 percent per year, compared to 3.2 percent for the United States, 2.8 percent for West Germany and 1.8 percent for Britain. In the 1980s growth has been lower in all the advanced

Annual Economic Growth Rates (percentages)				
	France	West Germany	Britain	U.S.
1981	0.5	0.2	−1.2	1.9
1982	1.8	−0.6	1.0	−2.5
1983	0.7	1.8	3.4	3.6
1984	1.5	3.0	3.0	6.4
1985	1.4	2.5	3.5	2.7
1986	2.0	2.8	2.3	2.5

countries, but France has done worse than its principal European competitors and the United States. French unemployment, which had been traditionally very low compared to the United States, West Germany and Britain, has been unprecedentedly and persistently high during these years of low economic growth.

There are three explanations for France's economic difficulties in this decade. First, the French GNP doubled in the period 1948–61 and again by 1973, and it could not be expected to go on growing at a comparable rate whatever policies were followed and whatever the external circumstances. In fact, the global economic environment became much less favorable for growth during the 1970s. The increase in energy prices after 1973 and 1979 induced a series of developments which contributed to lower growth than France, which imports three fourths of its energy supplies, had become accustomed to in the 1960s.

Second, there is general agreement that the Socialist government in its first year or two made a difficult situation worse by overestimating the economic strength of the country (including the supposed availability of "hidden" wealth that could be tapped for investment and social redistribution) and underestimating the duration of the international economic depression that coincided with its coming to power. At the same time, there is widespread agreement that the Socialists' second round of policies, beginning in mid-1982, put France back on the track to such recovery as it has achieved since.

Third, France has adjusted less well to the shocks of the last 15 years than West Germany and the United States for reasons that go deeper than the policy mistakes of 1981-82. Just when it had to export more to pay for its energy supplies, its industries not only faced increasing competition from newly industrializing Third World countries, as did those of all the industrial countries, but became less able to export on terms competitive with those of the United States, West Germany and Japan. In discussing this problem, the French recall that their industrial output, for reasons that are still debated and may still affect the economy today, grew more slowly in most of the 19th century and parts of the 20th than the output of, first, the British and then the Germans and Americans. There is a growing feeling in France that its remarkable modernization and development between World War II and the mid-1970s—the "30 glorious years"— were less thoroughgoing than had been thought and that some of the causes for earlier "lag" may persist. Evidence for this is diverse. Relatively few French companies count among the world's largest. The proportion of small businesses and farmers is large compared to other industrialized countries, and their productivity is lower. France habitually runs trade deficits—particularly in industrial goods—with other developed countries (with which West Germany, for example, runs surpluses) and tends to balance its accounts by surpluses with less-developed countries, including many in Africa with which it is linked by special postcolonial ties. This pattern suggests that France is less competitive on world markets than the most industrialized countries. Statistics for recent years show that this situation is getting worse.

In short, the relative efficiency of France's industry has declined just when the international economic system of the post-1973 period has become more sharply competitive. Explanations and prescriptions differ and are hotly debated. But in the face of these structural problems, few in France expect an early return to the employment and growth levels even of the 1970s, whatever policies are adopted. With a GNP of $710 billion in 1986, France still has a solid hold on the fifth rank in the world, far behind the United States, the Soviet Union and Japan, well behind West Germany ($902 billion), but well ahead of Britain ($555 billion) and Italy ($503 billion). Even so, some pessimists, looking at the record of the 1980s, go so far as to call France, once again, "the sick man of Europe."

Solutions of the Left

The Socialist government elected in 1981 was committed to nationalizing a substantial segment of French industry and banking, the first such effort since the sizable nationalizations of the postwar period which had included, among other companies, the nation's gas, electricity and coal-mining concerns, the Renault automobile works, and the four largest banks. Beginning in 1982, therefore, the government expropriated (with compensation) all the shares of two large financial groups (Paribas and Suez), three dozen banks and six major industrial groups: Compagnie Générale d'Electricité (CGE), Compagnie Générale des Constructions Téléphoniques and Thomson-Brandt (all involved in electrical and electronic engineering), Saint-Gobain (parachemicals and construction materials), and Rhone-Poulenc and Péchiney-Ugine-Kuhlman (chemicals). It also bought the two French subsidiaries of ITT and majority or controlling shares in several other industrial and financial concerns, including the arms-producing sections of Marcel Dassault and Matra, and the steel groups Sacilor and Usinor, which had been the recipients of large government loans. The newly nationalized concerns and those nationalized earlier accounted for 22 percent of all employment in France, 29 percent of all sales, 52 percent of all investment and 84 percent of all bank credit.

The primary motive behind these nationalizations was ideological. It is the traditional belief of the Socialists that the major means of production of the country should be publicly rather than privately owned, in part because this would reduce the influence of the "possessing classes" on economic and political life, in part because nationalized concerns, if managed to serve national rather than private interests, could lead the way in developing new forms of labor-management relations more responsive to the needs of their employees. In addition, however, some Socialists thought from the beginning—and this was increasingly emphasized as the economic situation worsened—that the state-owned industries, if better managed, could serve another urgent purpose: to be the cutting edge for increasing French productivity, output and exports, particularly in the high technology fields.

The government's industrial policy called for the nationalized concerns to be reorganized and for investment to be poured into them so that they might become more competitive in advanced products on international markets as well as "recapture the internal market" in fields being lost to imports. Private industry was to be helped to the same ends. By reshaping industry so as to both increase exports in lines where France could have a competitive advantage (the emphasis of the Giscard-Barre government) *and* reduce imports by producing goods that could at least compete more effectively at home, France would be able to improve its trade and payments balances. Stepping up domestic production also served the Socialists' interest in halting or slowing the decline in industrial employment. By directing resources to both public and private industries more rapidly and efficiently than the private owners of these companies might have done, the government hoped to revive some of the faltering "lame duck" lines of production that could not compete well either abroad or at home and expand such rapidly growing fields as computers, telecommunications and aerospace.

The restructuring programs that followed nationalization consolidated branches of companies that produced electronics, computers, chemicals and other products in ways likely to increase French competitiveness. The government invested 40 billion francs in the nationalized companies. The process also led to a decision to reduce steel production by one third between 1983 and 1988—a courageous departure from the policy of coming to the rescue of troubled firms that could not produce profitably in order to save jobs.

For all the ideological importance of nationalizations and denationalizations for the left and right and the long-term importance for the economy of the performance of this very large sector of the national plant, public attention was much more focused during the period of Socialist rule on the bread-and-butter facts of unemployment, inflation and deficits (budgetary, trade and payments). On taking office, the government decided to try to deal with unemployment—and honor pledges to its present and hoped-for supporters—by stimulating internal consumption, that is, by classical Keynesian pump-priming. It therefore increased the minimum wage, as well as family allowances, old-age pensions and benefits to the handicapped. These expenses were only partly covered by increases in contributions to the social welfare funds. At the same time the government promoted job-sharing by reducing the workweek to 39 hours, without reducing salaries, as a first step toward an eventual reduction to 35 hours; prescribed a fifth week of paid vacation; reduced the age of retirement to 60 years and encouraged earlier retirement; devised training schemes to delay the entry of young people into the job market; and created some 180,000 public sector jobs in 1981-82. These labor policies were also intended to deal with the longer-term problem of a shrinking labor market. Hundreds of thousands of industrial jobs have vanished since the mid-1970s, under both conservative and Socialist governments. Some of the job loss reflects improved productivity. But, even if the hoped-for level of modernization of production takes place, the expanding "high tech" sector of the economy may well provide fewer jobs than the declining older industries.

Fueling Inflation

The government knew that with consumer prices already rising at a rate of 13.5 percent in 1980, its policy created a risk of further stimulating inflation. It should have known, and soon learned, that increased purchasing power would also increase the demand for imports at a time when the high dollar made many of them (including oil) more expensive in francs and when French inflation depressed exports, thereby seriously threatening the country's external balances. The government's overall assumption was that the stimulated revival of economic activity in France would go along with, or soon be followed by, a revival of activity in the United States, induced by the policies of the new Reagan

Administration, and of world trade, and that in those circumstances French production and exports would also rise sufficiently to limit the worst consequences of reflation at home.

This assumption was not limited to wishful Socialist politicians, but it turned out to be wrong. The United States pursued a policy of high interest rates and severe deflation to deal with soaring inflation just when the French government decided to risk higher inflation in order to reduce unemployment. France would have been seriously affected by the deep global recession that followed, whatever its own policies. The countermovement it attempted could not be sustained. It then became clear, ironically, even to those who did not want to believe it, that France's integration into the world economy since 1945 (exports were 19 percent of its GNP in 1985) had been so successful that it could not establish socialism at home, or even try to pursue recovery by itself for very long, without rupturing its international ties (not least with the European Economic Community) and risking a loss of competitive efficiency and eventual impoverishment. Few politicians were willing to accept those risks.

Unemployment increased only slightly in 1982, and the economic growth rate, which had fallen to 0.5 percent in 1981, rose to 1.8 percent. But the price of these modest achievements was continuing high inflation and a deterioration of French international balances. As French reserves shrank, the government tried to deal with the problem by devaluing the franc in October 1981, but by too little in light of the fact that French prices were running ahead of West Germany's. By June 1982, when attempts to persuade the United States to reduce interest rates had failed, France had to devalue again, by 5.75 percent, in concert with a West German revaluation of the deutsche mark by 4.25 percent. This at least reestablished the pre-1980 relationship between the French and West German currencies, but a year late. A freeze on prices and wages was also imposed but no attempt was made to limit imports. As the U.S. recession continued and world interest rates remained high, France found itself, by March 1983, obliged to devalue once again (by 2.5 percent, together with a West German revaluation of 5.5 percent). This time it had to abandon the policy of internal reflation and adopt a set of austerity measures, including increased taxes and charges for public services and a slowdown in the growth of government spending. These were designed to reduce demand and rein in the budgetary and external deficits, even at the cost of higher unemployment.

This hard decision and the new "policy of rigor," which could not be presented as anything other than a sharp change in priorities, was preceded by a debate within the government in which some of President Mitterrand's advisers argued for a bolder course: to cut France loose at least temporarily from the European Community, the European Monetary System and other international economic commitments and resort to protectionism and stricter economic controls. Such steps were necessary, they claimed, to limit imports, insulate France from the negative effects of high international interest rates and so try to preserve the former domestic policy priorities. But the president decided that growth could not be achieved in this way. Nor was he willing to take the political as well as economic risks of slow or no growth which he saw in such a go-it-alone policy. To the consternation of the more ideologically minded Socialists, the government decided to pay the price—in order to reap the eventual benefits—of France's continued participation in the international economic system. It did so even at the cost of giving up many of the economic and social priorities with which the Socialists had come into office and admitting that there could be no "rupture" with capitalism in France while France remained, inevitably, a part of the capitalist world system.

Many observers consider that the "education" of the Socialists by adversity, which preceded this turnaround, and the apparent acceptance of this decision by the party and by most of the party's supporters in the 1986 elections signal both the end of utopianism on the French left concerning the possibility of replacing capitalism with some other system and an important step toward the formation of a broad consensus in France on the essentials of a realistic policy to deal with the country's difficult long-term economic problems.

The decisions of March 1983 and others that followed had political costs for the government: the ideological implications of the turnaround, the implicit admission that the policies followed in 1981–82 had been faulty, and, above all, the large jump in unemployment in 1984, and smaller increases in the following years, shocked many of its followers. But the decisions also had the desired economic benefits. Productivity increased; real wages did not. Growth fell to 0.7 percent in 1983 but then rose modestly to 1.5, 1.4 and 2.0 percent in the next three years. Most important, the balance of trade recovered by 1986 as the rate of increase of French consumer prices continued to decline (from 12.8 percent in 1981 to 5.5 percent in 1985) and, luckily for France, the international economic picture improved.

The new policies and their consequences, including a jump in unemployment from 8.5 percent in 1983 to 10 percent in 1984, were presented by the new prime minister, Laurent Fabius, who replaced Pierre Mauroy in July 1984, as essential to France's economic modernization. The Socialist party openly admitted that "constraints" inevitable in a democratic society had forced it to change course. Mitterrand said that wealth had to be created before it could be distributed. Competitiveness and its outward sign, profit making, have become part of the party's vocabulary, though it has not abandoned its commitment to the goal of social justice.

The period of Socialist rule ended with high unemployment (10.5 percent in 1986), which was an expected outcome of the policies followed since 1983. More positively, economic growth in 1986 was 2 percent, consumer prices rose only 2.2 percent, and France's foreign trade account was positive for the first time since 1978. But a principal cause of this improvement was the sharp fall in the price of petroleum and other raw materials. This not only reduced France's import bill but helped French manufacturers hold down their costs.

Far more ominous was the fact that France's surplus in trade of industrial goods fell by more than half in 1986, as compared to 1985, and the latter in turn was smaller than the 1984 surplus. The share of French exports in the total exports of the eight leading Western industrial nations was lower in 1985 (10.6 percent by volume) than in 1979 (11.5 percent), while West Germany's share grew in those years from 21.7 percent to 24 percent. Equally disquieting was the fact that French consumption increased by 3.3 percent in 1986 and, as in 1981-82, this led to an increase of 8 percent in imports of capital goods and 15 percent in consumer goods. The foreign penetration of the French market in manufactured goods was 32.5 percent in 1979 and 40.8 percent in 1985.

Solutions of the Right

The Chirac government, in pursuit of its long-term commitment to reinvigorate French business, which welcomed its victory in 1986, has cut taxes, limited wage and price controls, liberalized foreign exchange controls and made it easier for employers to dismiss workers without official authorization (a major goal of French business). It has also begun the multi-year process of selling to private buyers 65 companies, those taken over by the state after 1982 as well as some nationalized after World War II. Private capital has been much more eager to buy the offered shares than many had expected, and the government takes pride in the success of its "popular capitalism"—the purchase of shares by an unprecedentedly large number of small investors.

Profits in French industry have risen since 1984 and are expected to continue to do so in 1987 but business has used them not only for investment but to reduce its heavy indebtedness at high rates of interest. Research and development, which together with investment are the keys to restoring competitiveness to France's industrial system, have also lagged. Chirac at first cut spending on R & D but then recognized the need to do more.

Major economic indicators are projected to be worse in 1987 than in 1986. Growth is expected to increase by only about 1.25 percent. Inflation in France is expected to rise by about 3.25 percent in 1987 (compared to 0.2 percent in West Germany). Unemployment, which has increased every year since 1983, is projected to rise to more than 11 percent in 1987 and to 12 percent in 1988—election year. This is not surprising in face of the fact that French industrial production in 1986 was one percent less than it had been in 1980, while in those years industrial production increased by 15.1 percent in the United States, 9.6 percent in Britain and 7.2 percent in West Germany. The rise in French internal demand has stimulated imports more than internal production. The steady decline of France's position as an exporter of industrial products and the increasing penetration of the home market were not corrected by Socialist policies and have continued under the Chirac government. The structural problems of the French economy remain very serious. It is unclear to what extent some of the policies of the Socialist or conservative governments have laid the basis for improving the situation in the longer term.

The government scored what seemed to be a practical and psychological success in January 1987 when it persuaded West Germany to revalue its currency upward by 3 percent without insisting that France devalue. This would presumably help French exports vis-à-vis German while limiting the risks of heating up inflation in France. But this episode showed the continued vulnerability of France's economic managers to external events. The sharp fall of the dollar, which took place at about the same time as the European Monetary System realignment, not only overshadowed that event but seemed to empty it of much of its potential benefit for France by making U.S. products more competitive on world markets.

Whether this is the case, whether France can avoid another devaluation as a spur to exports, and whether a devaluation would do much good, the governing parties will have to fight the 1988 election with the argument that they need a full presidential term and full control of the government in order to carry out the reinvigoration of the French economy which they, like the Socialists before them, have pledged to bring about. Whether the voters have more confidence in them or in the Socialists to implement that pledge will be an important factor in the next election. But the need to get the economy moving is an urgent priority for whoever rules France if the country is to maintain its standard of living and its rank—economic and political—in the world.

4

Promoting the National Interest

The foreign policy pursued by the conservative French government since March 1986 has been practically identical to that followed by the Socialist government. This is not because the new prime minister and majority have deferred to the supposed "reserved domain" of Socialist President Mitterrand with respect to foreign and defense policies. This much discussed notion has only tenuous foundations in the constitution and originally reflected the fact that General de Gaulle was more interested in these matters than in domestic policy. On the contrary, Prime Minister Chirac believes that the constitutional provision which gives the government authority to "make and conduct the policy of the nation" applies to foreign as well as domestic affairs. If foreign and defense issues were not very important in the 1981 and 1986 campaigns, and are not likely to be in 1988, and if there has been essential continuity of policy with respect to them, the main reason is that there is a genuine consensus about them in France. This includes the Socialists and the two large parties of the right.

It is customary to describe this consensus as Gaullist, which implies that its objectives and methods are those of the general, adapted to changing circumstances. In his own time there was no consensus but bitter dispute about his policies, which were assertively presented as if deliberately to provoke contention. Many in France opposed his decisions to develop nuclear weapons, take France out of the Atlantic alliance's system of military integration, veto Britain's application for membership in the European Economic Community, block further European integration and open a dialogue with the Soviet Union aimed, it seemed, at loosening up the two blocs in Europe and reducing the influence of the two superpowers.

Consensus and Continuity

Have the Mitterrand and Chirac governments pursued these policies? Yes and no.

Some of de Gaulle's attitudes and decisions, once very controversial in France, have now become institutionalized to such an extent, with the support of the mainstream parties, that they are practically beyond policy discussion.

● Everyone is for French "independence" in the sense so often asserted by the general: France can and should make its own decisions with respect to its vital interests and should not have decisions imposed on it by the supranational institutions of the European Community or the overweening power of the United States. While the United States is an indispensable ally, its tendency to assert authority over France must be resisted. Commitment to independence has, in fact, become so established in France that it is scarcely mentioned in official rhetoric any more. Neither the Socialist nor the Chirac government made a point of affirming France's independence to its own people or to other countries in the provocative ways that de Gaulle relished and thought necessary in order to raise French self-confidence after the many difficult years following 1940. French politicians of both left and right act, on the whole, as if that battle had been won. They find it safe now to note the importance to France of both the European Economic Community and the North Atlantic Treaty Organization (NATO) without fear of being denounced for undermining French independence. The French are much less aggressively defensive than formerly even with respect to their language and culture, which play an important part in their sense of national independence and influence. Jack Lang, the Socialist minister of culture, could warn the world in 1982 to resist American "cultural imperialism," which, he said, seized not territory but consciousness. Five years later a government dominated by the political heirs of de Gaulle could proudly complete a deal for building the first European Disneyland near Paris.

• All parties, except the Communists, have accepted the existence and modernization of the French nuclear force and purely national control of it as both a prerequisite and a corollary of France's independence. There is discussion about strategy and weapons systems but none about the fact that France is and should remain a nuclear military power. The nuclear force, once opposed by the United States and by some in France who feared that it would diminish France's security by isolating it from the Western defense system, has long since been endorsed by the alliance itself (in the Ottawa declaration of June 1974) as a useful supplement to the deterrent capability of American (and British) nuclear weapons.

• At the same time few in France call for France's return to NATO military integration. It is understood that cooperative arrangements and contingency plans have been worked out between France and the alliance by de Gaulle himself and his successors. Crossing the line to return to integration, which would mean agreeing to place French forces automatically under alliance command in wartime, is considered unnecessary and therefore not worth the debate which such reversal of policy after more than 20 years would require.

• De Gaulle managed to preserve close security, political, economic and cultural ties with most of France's colonies even as he agreed to their independence in the years 1960–62. Practically no one in France challenges the maintenance of these special relationships, the assignment to these countries of the bulk of France's economic and technical assistance, the stationing of troops in some of them and even their occasional use to protect African allies from invasion (as in Chad) or domestic challenges.

President Giscard, in the Gaullist tradition, tried to preserve the "special" French-Soviet relationship. Under Mitterrand and Chirac, France's relations with the Soviet Union have been distant.

French Embassy Press & Information Division

• Closely connected with this is the notion, also developed by de Gaulle, that France has a special role to play with respect to the countries of the Third World because of its unique position as a member of the Western alliance but not a member of a U.S.-led military bloc. More was said about this by the Socialists than by their successors. But French parties of both the right and left hold that France can give the Third World countries, beginning with the ex-colonies in Africa but not limited to them, an "option" other than that of becoming pawns in the U.S.-Soviet competition. France offers them a model and a source of economic aid and arms.

Consensus and Change

If French policy were confined to these important items, it could well be called Gaullist. But it is not. The circumstances of the 1980s are not the same as those of the 1960s. The opportunities and constraints which France faces in the international arena are different. French policies are muted in some important areas where the general was outspoken and are aligned with U.S.

policy on others where he opposed it. Yet there is nearly as broad a consensus on these departures from Gaullism, even in the Gaullist party, as there is continued solid support, even in the Socialist party, for the apparently untouchable foundations of French foreign policy.

The main focus of France's external policy must always be its relations with the superpowers and the impact of their relations with each other on Europe, the area of greatest importance to France. President Mitterrand took office at a time when the East-West *détente*—of which General de Gaulle had been one of the fathers or prophets and which had developed during the 1970s—was crumbling away, to be followed by renewed high tension between the United States and the Soviet Union. President Giscard, in a classic Gaullist response, had tried to halt the deterioration of superpower relations in 1980, or at least to distance France—and Western Europe—from it, by meeting with Soviet President Leonid I. Brezhnev in Warsaw, at a time when the United States was urging its allies to impose sanctions of various kinds on the U.S.S.R. because of its invasion of Afghanistan. Giscard found that his gesture, besides being ineffectual, cost him support at home.

Mitterrand, on the other hand, announced that French-Soviet relations could not be normal as long as Soviet troops remained in Afghanistan. This abandonment of the fact or pretense of a "special" French-Soviet relationship as a key element in France's independent foreign policy was popular at home, where both intellectual and public opinion had become very critical of the Soviet Union. Neither the Mitterrand government nor the opposition, including the Gaullist party, nor the French public seemed concerned that this distancing of France from the Soviet Union implied the end, at least for a time, of its long-standing posture of trying to maintain a certain balance between the superpowers. This, in turn, implied a reidentification of France with the U.S.-led Western alliance at a time, in the early 1980s, when renewed East-West tension was repolarizing Europe. Reducing that polarization had, of course, been a major goal of de Gaulle's policy and, to a lesser extent, that of his successors.

In 1984 Mitterrand visited the Soviet Union and Chirac did so in 1987. But French relations with the Soviets have remained distant, and no attempt has been made, by Mitterrand or Chirac, to suggest that there is a serious dialogue going on between the two governments. Nor has either of them had much to say about the great Gaullist objective of "overcoming Yalta" (the French code phrase for reuniting divided Europe). This rhetorical centerpiece of Gaullist diplomacy seems far from the minds of French policymakers in the 1980s. So far, at least, they have not found in the policies of Mikhail S. Gorbachev what de Gaulle saw, or claimed to see, in Soviet policies 20 years ago: prospects for a loosening of Soviet control over Eastern Europe and, thus, for reducing the division between the two parts of the Continent and the dependence of both on the superpowers.

Nowhere was the French evolution from "balance" to Western solidarity more clearcut than with respect to West Germany. In January 1983 Mitterrand visited that country and, in a much noted speech to the Bundestag, in effect told the West Germans—then in the midst of an election campaign—to vote for those parties which would reaffirm their country's solidarity with the Atlantic alliance by going ahead with the planned deployment of intermediate-range nuclear forces (INF). Since deployment had been endorsed by Chancellor Helmut Kohl's Christian Democrats and their Free Democrat partners in government but not by the divided Social Democrats, Mitterrand thus urged the West Germans not only to do what the United States wanted and the Soviet Union opposed but to keep out of office the German counterparts of his own Socialist party.

This, too, was popular in France, where the idea that the West Germans might break loose from their Atlantic alliance moorings on the INF issue, or any other, in order to pursue neutralism or reunification was profoundly disturbing. The rise of what some described as German Gaullism had the effect of undercutting traditional French Gaullism. Where de Gaulle had urged West Germany to follow France's lead in improving relations with the Soviets and distancing itself from overdependence on the United States, Mitterrand in effect counseled the opposite.

Efforts were made to reassure the West Germans that French military power was behind them in their resistance to Soviet pressure with respect to INF deployment and on a broader scale as well. A long-dormant article of the 1963 French-German friendship treaty was reactivated as the basis for consultations on defense. New projects were launched for bilateral (and multilateral) production of weapons. The recently formed French rapid action force (FAR) was described as being available for emergencies in West Germany as well as elsewhere. The French have never gone so far as to extend an explicit nuclear guarantee to West Germany, but they have emphasized their belief that their own security was closely entwined with that of West Germany. In one of the typically ambiguous statements with which French officials address this subject, François Fillon, president of the National Assembly's defense committee, said that French-German cooperation "does not mean that the defense of France is extended to the Elbe but that we are disposed to have sufficient means and to use them to support our allies in their combat." Let the West Germans, and optimists with respect to European defense cooperation, find such comfort in that as they can.

On the most important European security issue of the 1980s, therefore, France, with little internal debate, placed itself squarely alongside the United States and Atlantic solidarity and athwart not only Soviet policy but also the aspirations of the groups in many countries which might have welcomed French leadership in pursuit of greater independence for the European countries, West and East, from the ups and downs of U.S.-Soviet relations. The French government which took this position included, it will be remembered, four Communist members, who did not like the policy but preferred accepting it to leaving the cabinet. The United States, for its part, appreciated French support on this key issue enough to avoid, on the whole, being overly disturbed by the four Communists or offended by disagreements with France on other issues.

There were many such issues. Enhanced French Atlanticism under the Mitterrand government in no way implied any diminution of France's attachment to its independent defense policy and nuclear force, which in fact was being strengthened; its independent position within the alliance; or its willingness to hold and express policy positions unwelcome to the United States. Thus, it strongly and successfully resisted a U.S. effort to oblige France (and also West Germany, Britain and Italy) to give up a long-planned project to buy natural gas from the Soviet Union. In its first years the Mitterrand government vigorously criticized U.S. policy in Central America. Less was heard of this from the Socialists as time passed, however, and nothing from the Chirac government.

The Mitterrand government strongly endorsed the Reagan Administration's buildup of U.S. military forces as necessary to reestablishing the global strategic balance. But it opposed the Strategic Defense Initiative (SDI) as another long step in the arms race. Less openly, it opposed SDI as a threat to the credibility of the American guarantee to Western Europe and also of the French nuclear force should U.S. development of an antimissile defense system lead the U.S.S.R. to do the same. The Socialists, however, did not prevent French companies from taking part in SDI development, and the Chirac government ended official hostility to the project. It, in turn, was not happy with the ambiguous outcome of the Reagan-Gorbachev summit meeting in Iceland in late 1986 or with the prospect of a U.S.-Soviet agreement to remove intermediate-range and short-range missiles from Europe. In this the French have been careful to show sympathy for West German concerns on this topic, so as not to let West Germany feel isolated among its allies. But they have been careful also not to seem to be taking the lead of a European bloc which would actively oppose U.S. policy. A hasty criticism of such an agreement as a "European Munich" by defense minister André Giraud was repudiated by Chirac. France has thus been no more willing to use the issue of missile removal to raise European consciousness in face of the United States (concerned though it is by the prospect) than it had been earlier to use the issue of missile deployment in that way. Both the Socialist and conservative governments have insisted that French nuclear weapons must not be the subject of superpower arms control negotiations or be included (as the Russians at first insisted) in an eventual agreement to limit or remove intermediate-range missiles in Europe.

The Socialist government was continuously critical of U.S. economic policy, which maintained high budget deficits and high interest rates to the detriment, it was said, of growth in other countries. Chirac has had less to say on these matters, in part because U.S. economic policies have changed somewhat. But the rapid fall of the dollar in 1987 was no more welcome to the conservative government than the high dollar was to its predecessor.

Europe and Beyond

While expressing solidarity with the United States on most East-West security issues, the Socialist government tried to promote greater European cooperation on these and other questions, in part to assert traditional French leadership in this area, in part to strengthen this established framework for French-German cooperation. Mitterrand took a strong personal role in reaching an agreement in 1984 to end the long dispute about Britain's share in financing the European Economic Community budget, which had held up progress in other areas. Subsequently there was much talk, in France as elsewhere, that with this obstacle at last removed and with agreement also with respect to the admission of Spain and Portugal, the Community could move on to closer economic, political and diplomatic unity. Mitterrand, who has said that "France is our country, Europe is our future," continued to identify himself with "Europe," most conspicuously by proposing Eureka (the European Research Agency), a united effort by the European countries to keep abreast of advanced technology in order to avoid falling increasingly behind the United States and Japan.

Hopes for more rapid European progress have been realized only to a limited degree. The failure of the European countries to achieve a united or even coordinated response to SDI is a striking indication of how far they still are from being able to speak with one voice to the United States even on a matter of the highest strategic, political and economic importance to all of them. They do better with respect to trade and, to some extent, monetary issues. But the principal European countries, including France, still pursue distinctive national foreign policies.

The ideological quarrel over European integration which divided the French in the 1960s is dead. But so, it seems, is enthusiasm for integration. Neither right nor left advocates moving toward the kind of European federalism that was talked about by Jean Monnet and many others in the 1950s, when the European Economic Community was launched as the keystone of what was expected to be an ever-widening unity. European institutions and cooperation are important to all French governments for practical and political reasons. But none has recently made the kind of ostentatious attempt to lead and speak for Europe that de Gaulle did. Optimists point to the decision of the Community members to establish a real common market by 1992—only 35 years after the treaty providing for a common market was signed. But even if this happens, the Community would still be far from having common economic policies and farther from common foreign and defense policies. "Europe" is still a distant goal and is likely to remain so, as far as French policy is concerned, for the foreseeable future.

There has also been essential continuity in French policy with respect to the Third World and, in particular, France's ties with Africa. The Socialists had talked of "moralizing" France's African policy, which implied using aid to require reforms by the more notoriously dictatorial and corrupt regimes. But little came of this. The Socialists were also no more hesitant than their predecessors to use armed force to maintain French interests. Thus, they sent troops to Chad in 1983 to help the government resist an advance by Libyans and Libyan-backed Chadians long in control of the northern part of the country. France withdrew its forces in 1984 after a somewhat mysterious negotiation with Libya but sent them back the next year when it became obvious that Libya had not withdrawn its own forces as promised. French aid to the Chadians played an important part when they routed Libyan forces from the northern part of the country in 1987.

The Socialists, as a party, traditionally had better relations with Israel than the French conservative governments, and Mitterrand became the first French president to visit that country. His call for a Palestinian state on the West Bank as part of a peace settlement and for including the Palestine Liberation Organization in negotiations did not improve his government's standing with Israel or advance the peace process. The important French position in Lebanon has dwindled along with those of other Western countries, including the United States. Whereas the Socialists provided arms and aid to Iraq in its long war with Iran, the Chirac government, while continuing to do the same, in one of its few departures from Socialist policy tried to improve French relations with Iran, presumably with the hope that the Tehran government might help in the release of French hostages held in Lebanon and limit the depredations of Middle East terrorists in France itself. Instead, relations worsened and were officially broken in July 1987. The Chirac government also maintained the continuity of France's independent and supportive position with respect to the Third World by publicly refusing permission to the United States for American planes to fly over French territory on their bombing raid against Libya in April 1986.

Strategy for Security

French foreign policy has been largely consistent and reasonably successful during the 1980s. At the same time the government has been more circumspect than in de Gaulle's time about proclaiming either ambitious long-term foreign policy goals ("overcoming Yalta") or the importance of France as a global power. Its defense policy, however, has remained consistent with that of the general in that it is designed both to assure the security of France from attack and to underpin the independent posture which is the point of departure for the country's claim to major-power rank. These are ambitious, and expensive, objectives. Since the resources which even an expanding French economy can provide for defense purposes are limited—and economic growth has been low in the 1980s—the French have had to choose carefully how to invest the money available for defense. In this decade they have spent about 4 percent of GNP every year for that purpose (compared to 3.3 percent, in 1985, for West Germany, 5.2 percent for Britain and 6.6 percent for the United States).

The basis of General de Gaulle's security policy was that France had to have credible means to deter a Soviet attack. To this end it needed nuclear warheads, vehicles for delivering them against targets in the Soviet Union, and a doctrine for their use that would persuade the Soviet government that France could and would retaliate with these weapons if its "supreme interests" were threatened.

France remained a member of the Atlantic alliance even after de Gaulle withdrew French forces from its military wing in 1966 and asked the alliance to remove its headquarters and installations from French territory. But he asserted that, once the Soviet Union had developed the capability to inflict heavy damage on U.S. soil in the 1960s, the American guarantee to Western Europe, which was the basis of the alliance, lost credibility. France therefore had no choice but to provide for its own security in the way he proposed. It is likely that he would have pursued the same policy even if the U.S.-Soviet strategic balance had remained unchanged. He was convinced that a nation's possession of an independent nuclear force was the badge of major-power status in the late 20th century. Possessing such weapons made France at least the peer of Britain, which already had them, and kept it ahead of West Germany in the rank order of nations.

De Gaulle of course knew that France could not hope to build a nuclear arsenal equal to that of the United States or the Soviet Union. French strategic doctrine therefore had to be designed to demonstrate, to the Russians as well as to others who at first did not take French nuclear weapons very seriously as either a security system or a status symbol, that France could in fact deter Soviet attack. To this end a theory of proportionate response was devised (sometimes called the tear-off-an-arm doctrine). In brief, the French government argued that, while its nuclear force could not aspire to damage the U.S.S.R. to the extent that the United States might, these weapons could nevertheless inflict injury on

Soviet cities so grievous that Russian decisionmakers would be deterred from attacking France. They would realize that even the total destruction of France, which was within their power technically, would bring them no benefit proportionate to the losses they would suffer from an inevitable French nuclear response. Since the French doctrine, in its original version, claimed that nuclear weapons would be used only in response to an attack on France, the Russians were put on notice that the "sanctuary" of French territory would be defended by nuclear weapons, if necessary, even against attack by conventional forces.

The credibility of this and other such theories depended, of course, on the effectiveness of the weapons systems France could build. The first generation, made up of Mirage bombers, was criticized in the 1960s on the grounds that the planes were not likely to be able to penetrate Soviet air defenses to deliver their nuclear bombs. The French answered, however, that the Russians could not be sure that none would get through and were therefore deterred. In the atmosphere of oncoming détente in the late 1960s and 1970s, strategic debate of this kind was considerably muted. France's claims to status by reason of its nuclear deterrent capability came gradually to be accepted as meaningful if not wholly convincing to everyone. In any case that capability remained untested, as de Gaulle was wise enough to have foreseen. France, after all, had no common frontier with the Soviet Union and no bilateral dispute with it. War between them was most unlikely except in the case of a general war in Europe which would involve many countries near France that remained within the military system of the alliance and contained U.S. bases and forces. This system, whatever might be said about the credibility of the American guarantee, continued to be seen by many Europeans, and presumably by the Russians too, as an effective deterrent against Soviet attack or pressure.

The French nevertheless have worked to make their nuclear force more effective, curtailing the numbers and equipment of their conventional forces to keep overall military spending at a generally fixed proportion of the national product. Forty modern Mirage bombers armed with nuclear weapons remain deployed.

The second generation nuclear system was a group of 18 ground-to-ground ballistic missiles located on the Plateau d'Albion in southeast France. These have always been considered vulnerable, which is why no more were deployed. But they too still remain operational and there are plans to "harden" them or make them more secure against a Soviet strike.

The third generation and heart of the French deterrent capability is a group of nuclear-powered ballistic missile submarines. There are now six of these and one more is to be ready in about 1994. Whereas the first five were equipped with 16 missiles apiece, each carrying one nuclear warhead, the 16 missiles on the sixth will each carry six warheads mounted on multiple independently targetable reentry vehicles (MIRVs). Four of the older submarines are to be retrofitted with such multiwarhead missiles. When that has been done, the six French submarines will carry no less than 496 warheads—a very impressive expansion of France's deterrent capability. The Chirac government's 1987–91 military program anticipates that the number of warheads on each missile will be increased from six to nine by the end of the century. These modern submarines are likely to remain invulnerable to Soviet attack for many years, barring major breakthroughs in the effectiveness of antisubmarine warfare.

In addition to these strategic systems, French Super Etendard carrier aircraft are armed with air-to-ground nuclear missiles. A nuclear-powered carrier has been approved, to be built over 10 years. There are also 30 or more launchers for the Pluton ground-to-ground theater or tactical missiles (with a range of 120 kilometers) and a longer-range follow-on, the Hades (with a 350 kilometer range), is being developed. French officials have said that research on the development of enhanced radiation weapons ("neutron bombs") has been successfully completed. But no decision to produce and deploy them has been announced. They may be placed on the Hades missile. The place of these "pre-strategic" weapons in France's deterrent strategy remains unclear. Their availability implies that France wants a capability to use nuclear weapons otherwise than in the ultimate "battle of France" which the strategic nuclear force is meant to deter.

Notwithstanding the emphasis placed on its nuclear systems, France also maintains substantial conventional forces with a variety of missions. France has a long-established tradition of universal (male) military service, which is supported by both the right and left and challenged by almost no one. The period of service is now 12 months. The armed forces comprise about 558,000 uniformed personnel, of which 296,000 are in the army. Some 50,000 are stationed in West Germany, not under NATO command but on the basis of a bilateral French-German agreement reached when France left alliance military integration in 1966. There are 2,700 French troops in West Berlin in accordance with France's participation, along with the United States and Britain, in the "occupation" and defense of the city. A special rapid action force of 45,000 personnel has been created in the last decade to allow France to send well-trained forces on short notice to areas of crisis or tension, whether West Germany, Africa or elsewhere. Over 21,000 members of all services are stationed in France's overseas departments and territories in the West Indies, the Indian Ocean and the Pacific. More than 9,000 are stationed in six African countries, once colonies, with which France has close ties: Djibouti, the Central African Republic, Chad, Senegal, Gabon and the Ivory Coast.

Are Changes Needed?

France's future security planning has to take account of developments between the superpowers with respect to strategic defense systems and arms control. There has been debate in France in recent years, like that in other Western countries, about whether its own forces and strategy, and the alliance's, need to be changed in light of changing strategic and other considerations. There has been, however, no large antinuclear weapons movement, as in West Germany and Britain, and little support for such concepts as Western renunciation of the first use or early use of nuclear weapons (which would, of course, undermine French strategy). France's lack of nervousness about plans for the use of nuclear weapons, compared with many of its neighbors, is explained by the French as reflecting the fact that their possession of a national nuclear force gives them such confidence in their own security as to immunize them from the kind of doubts and fears which have fed "peace movements" in countries whose security depends on the changeable United States—sometimes too passive, sometimes too belligerent.

There has also been little support for the idea that France should expand its conventional forces (instead of reducing them) in order to make early recourse to nuclear weapons in a European war less likely. To the French this sounds like a prescription for paying more for less security and status. Nor has there been much support for cutting back France's military commitments and presence outside Europe. The Chirac government's military law, adopted in 1987 with the support of all parties except the Communists, provides essentially for continuity in the basic structure of French defense policy.

Discussion of possible changes in French security policy has focused on whether France should extend a nuclear guarantee in some way to West Germany and how it should promote greater cooperation among the European allies with respect to strategic planning and weapons production in the face of the dominant position the United States now holds in these fields. A considerable number of weapons have been developed over the last decades by French-German or multilateral European consortia. But the idea of somehow bringing West Germany under the French nuclear umbrella, while increasingly talked about by French politicians and defense specialists, has never led to any concrete move. This is the case mainly because whatever credibility there is in the contention that France would risk nuclear war to defend itself could not be convincingly extended to West German or other territory. There is also reason to doubt that the West Germans would find such a French guarantee much of a supplement to the allegedly defective one the United States has provided for four decades. Would the Germans believe that the French would be more willing to sacrifice Paris for Hamburg than the United States would be to sacrifice New York? Would the Germans believe that the Russians would believe it? Proposals to station French nuclear-armed forces nearer Germany's eastern border have also not found much support, for the same reason. Moreover, such action would seem to deprive France of its hallowed theoretical option of deciding whether or not to become involved in a European war, if that should break out, and whether and when to use French nuclear weapons.

President Mitterrand restated the obvious when he said, in January 1987, that "the nuclear arm is not divisible" and that European political unity was a prerequisite for a European defense community. Defense Minister Giraud took the same position when he said, in April, that France had the armaments it needed but that "it would be ridiculous to think that by itself France could assure the covering of one or another European country or part of Europe." That being the French position, it is possible to envisage closer consultations among various European countries on defense problems and common production of weapons by various groupings, but not, in the foreseeable future, a "European" nuclear force or protective system based on French weapons. Chancellor Kohl has said that he understands that the French nuclear umbrella cannot be extended to West Germany.

French authorities talk less these days about their country's independence as compared to years past, and cooperation—including contingency planning between France and the alliance—is understood to be significant. But France seems unlikely to give up this long established basis of its policy in favor of any alternative which might weaken, rather than reinforce, the credibility of its claim to be able to deter Soviet attack on French vital interests as France alone defines them. On that claim rests much more than a projected line of action in the event of war in Europe. French leaders of both right and left remain Gaullist in their belief that French morale, self-confidence and national cohesion depend to a very considerable extent on public belief in the ability of the country to defend itself by its own will and means and to protect its interests in a dangerous world.

5

What's Next?

The presidential election in France will take place in April 1988 unless President Mitterrand leaves office before then. Prime Minister Chirac, who intends to seek the presidency, presumably accepted office in March 1986 because he believed that its high visibility and his achievements as leader of the victorious conservative coalition would give him an advantage. This advantage was assumed to outweigh the inevitable difficulties of dealing with France's problems and the risks of political misadventure arising from unforeseeable sources. In fact, his government's clash with the students in December 1986 and the strikes that followed cost him support in the polls which he has not regained.

Chirac's political strategy of trying to win over Jean-Marie Le Pen's followers by addressing their concerns about immigration and security does not seem to have worked. But it has created divisions in the governing parties. Critics accuse the prime minister of sacrificing principle (and risking the votes of centrist voters) in an attempt to co-opt the extreme right. On the other hand, some parliamentarians of the majority already foresee that they themselves will need help from Le Pen's followers to win elections. They have begun to signal to their leaders that if these voters cannot be won away from the FN, as seems to be the case, then it will be necessary to consider how to do business with Le Pen.

Former prime minister Raymond Barre is waiting quietly out of office in the hope that he will be the strongest conservative candidate on the first ballot of the presidential election (particularly if Le Pen draws a substantial number of votes away from Chirac). Then, as the sole standard-bearer of the right, he would hope to defeat the Socialist candidate in the runoff—provided that a sizable number of Chirac's followers do not defect, as in 1981, from a candidate who is conservative but not of their party.

President Mitterrand's standing in opinion polls has also risen since March 1986, as has that of the Socialist party. He is in a strong position to seek reelection in 1988 if he chooses to do so. If he does not, former agriculture minister Michel Rocard seems to have received Mitterrand's blessing despite years of feuding and is likely to be the Socialist candidate. Rocard has been a popular figure in the country, if less so in his party, for many years, having identified himself with the kind of pragmatic policies which the Socialists—and Mitterrand—once rejected in principle but, after 1982, adopted in practice. Polls suggest that he would be well placed to challenge whichever candidate of the right runs best on the first ballot.

Most votes will probably be cast on the basis of party loyalty, the personalities of the candidates and economic issues rather than on constitutional grounds. But the outcome will of course affect how the constitution is applied after the election. If a president of the right is elected, he should be able to control the present National Assembly or, by dissolving it, bring about the election of another with a larger majority of the RPR and UDF. In either case he would be in a position to impose his choice for prime minister on the parties that dominated the National Assembly and thus reassert the presidential domination of the system which has been in abeyance since March 1986. Cohabitation will then appear to have been an exception, not so unsuccessful that it would be shunned in the future, but by no means the "normal" method of government of the Fifth Republic.

Drawing by Plantu

Reprinted from *Le Monde* in the *Manchester Guardian Weekly*, June 7, 1987

Immigration will be high up on the list of issues in the 1988 presidential election campaign if National Front leader Jean-Marie Le Pen has his way. He wants to limit the number of immigrants from North Africa, whose children are heavily represented among the more than one million foreign pupils currently enrolled in French schools.

If a Socialist is elected president, he would either have to accept limits on his authority like those imposed on Mitterrand by cohabitation with the conservative majority in the National Assembly, which seems most improbable after he has defeated the leaders of that majority, or he would have to enter into a struggle with the conservatives which, sooner rather than later, would require dissolution of the National Assembly before its normal termination in 1991 and new elections. (One of the arguments cited in favor of the view that Mitterrand will not seek reelection is that he would not be eager, at 72, to get into such a drawn-out and uncertain political conflict.) If the Socialists and their allies then won control of the Assembly, the dominance of the president would be reestablished. If the Socialists fell short of such control but were able to negotiate an alliance with a sufficient number of deputies from other parties (the centrist elements of the UDF are more likely candidates than the Communists), then the president could again dominate the system for as long as that alliance lasted, but within the policy and personnel constraints imposed on him by it.

If the conservatives won control of the Assembly again, then some form of cohabitation would have to be worked out. In that case, the president might have more real power than Mitterrand has had since March 1986 but less than he would have under the previous hypotheses. Constant bargaining and threats of new elections might define this version of cohabitation. The effectiveness of government would itself become a political issue. At some point the voters might have to pay more attention to that issue than they normally would. They could decide to reestablish presidential domination, as it existed under both right and left before 1986, by putting the two branches of government in the hands of one or the other political bloc. Or they could accept divided authority and its consequences, not just as an interim between elections but as a more lasting and probably less harmonious adaptation of the institutions of the Fifth Republic.

Whoever governs France after the next presidential election will face very difficult economic problems. The conservatives have not yet had time to implement their solutions fully and would presumably pursue them if elected. The Socialists, if returned to power, are not likely to go back to the policies of 1981–82 but to follow the more pragmatic course they adopted in 1983. All French governments will continue to find their options constrained by developments in the world economy, particularly those in the United States. They will also find that the hard choices required to achieve the maximum levels of growth, employment and prosperity permitted by the international economic situation may be unpopular in the near-term. Whether or not France has strong and coherent governments will have important consequences for its ability to implement effective economic policies.

Foreign and defense policies are less likely to be major political issues because of the substantial consensus that exists. But party positions and voter choices on domestic affairs will affect France's ability to conduct an effective foreign policy. For one thing, the country's prestige is linked to the coherence of its system of government—an advantage which the Fifth Republic has had during most of its existence, compared to the Fourth. For another, France's ability to finance its planned security program, maintain its relatively high level of foreign aid and preserve its independence from foreign lenders and creditors requires a reasonably sound economy. The relations of the superpowers—whether they move in the direction of tension or some kind of neo-détente—will, as always, profoundly affect the choices available to France for protecting and promoting its own perceived interests. France's foreign policy, like its economic affairs, will thus depend on both external circumstances largely outside its control and the ability of its political system—and the parties and leaders who control it—to make decisions.

Talking It Over

A Note for Students and Discussion Groups

This issue of the HEADLINE SERIES, like its predecessors, is published for every serious reader, specialized or not, who takes an interest in the subject. Many of our readers will be in classrooms, seminars or community discussion groups. Particularly with them in mind, we present below some discussion questions—suggested as a starting point only—and references for further reading.

Discussion Questions

How does France's long history of revolutions and other internal conflicts and divisions affect the ability of the French people to govern themselves and deal with their current problems?

What reasons are there to believe that the constitution of the Fifth Republic, now almost 30 years old, will provide a lasting structure of government for France? What reasons are there to doubt that?

What are the main features of the French system of government? the roles of the president, prime minister and parliament? of the political parties?

What were the principal objectives of the Socialist party when it took office in 1981? To what extent did it achieve its goals?

What were the policy objectives of the conservative parties that won the 1986 elections?

Why did the way the government worked change after the elections of March 1986?

How has the French party system changed since 1958? For what reasons?

What is the "immigration problem" and why is it a political issue?

What are the main problems of the French economy?

Why do the French people believe that their country should be and is a major power in European and world affairs?

In what ways does the consensus in France about foreign policy include elements of General de Gaulle's policies? In what ways does it differ from them?

Why are relations with West Germany so important to France?

Why do French governments both value their alliance with the United States and, at the same time, disagree with American policies in important ways? List some of those disagreements.

Why do the French believe that their nuclear forces can deter Soviet attack on France? What do you think about that?

In 1988 France will have a presidential election. How might the outcome affect foreign policy? How might it affect the way the system of government works?

READING LIST

Ardagh, John, *France in the 1980s.* New York, Penguin, 1983. A British journalist's comprehensive review of French life: economy, society, culture.

Balassa, Bela, "Five Years of Socialist Economic Policy in France: A Balance Sheet." *The Tocqueville Review,* Vol. 7 (1985–86). A detailed account of the Socialist party's economic record.

Cerny, Philip G., and Schain, Martin, eds., *Socialism, the State and Public Policy in France*. New York, Methuen, 1985. An analysis of the Socialist party's aims and achievements in power.

DePorte, A.W., "France's New Realism." *Foreign Affairs*, Autumn 1984. France's adaptation to the international problems of the 1980s.

Ehrmann, Henry W., *Politics in France*, 4th ed. Boston, Mass., Little, Brown, 1983. The roots, setting and structure of French politics.

Hoffmann, Stanley, "The Odd Couple." *The New York Review of Books*, September 25, 1986. The record of political cohabitation between Mitterrand and Chirac.

Rosenblum, Mort, *Mission to Civilize: The French Way*. New York, Harcourt Brace Jovanovich, 1986. An American journalist's survey of France and the French, old and new, from Quebec to Tahiti.

Wilson, Frank L., *French Political Parties Under the Fifth Republic*. New York, Praeger, 1982. A comprehensive discussion of the French party system.

Wright, Vincent, *The Government and Politics of France*, 2nd ed. New York, Holmes and Meier, 1983. Constitution, parties and decision-making in the Fifth Republic.

Yost, David S., "Radical Change in French Defense Policy?" *Survival*, January/February 1986. A comprehensive analysis of French security policy and proposals to change it.

Zeldin, Theodore, *France, 1848-1945*, 2 vols. London, Oxford University Press, 1973 and 1977. A large-scale analysis of the interplay in French society of ambition, love, politics, intellect, taste and anxiety.